# How to Be Silent

Martin Willitts, Jr.

FUTURECYCLE PRESS

*www.futurecycle.org*

Library of Congress Control Number: 2015952974

Published by FutureCycle Press
Lexington, Kentucky, USA

ISBN 978-1-938853-82-1

# Contents

## I. Silence Is the Pathway to Visions

## II. The Spiritual Journey

## III. Rapture!

## IV. The Temporary World

*The ecstatic poets wrote lovingly about the search for God.
And when they found God, they were overwhelmed with God's presence.
They reached out with praise, or psalms, or anguish, or tribulations,
or struggled with the unspeakable, or found they could not
give words to what they had seen or heard, but many
of the mystics saw God as Love.*

## I. Silence Is the Pathway to Visions

"You can hear the footsteps of God when silence reigns in the mind."

—Sri Sathya Sai Baba

"We need to find God, and he cannot be found in noise and restlessness. God is the friend of silence. See how nature—trees, flowers, grass— grows in silence; see the stars, the moon and the sun, how they move in silence.... We need silence to be able to touch souls."

—Mother Teresa

## How to Be Silent

Into the evening and beyond, swooping
nightjars chase moths. The sound of them,
less than silence, is hush-spiraling.
If this be the color of tree bark,
then what are those long-tipped wings
sliding across the moorlands out of the brackens—
with no more noise than a prayer kept to ourselves?
Nightjars conceal themselves from daylight,
and now they are after the large flying insects
like there is no tomorrow. And they should know,
belonging more to darkness than to the known,
moving with suddenness. Into the evening
and beyond, where light is already disappearing,
are whispers of sounds that are less than whispers.
*We* want to reduce the universe into simple concepts,
into a bird touching silence. We want distilled silence—
to reach into that speechless sense of wonder.
We want to suppress fears that worry at our bones.
Those darting nightjars, a smothering darkness,
stopping sounds into insignificance, shush the stars.
They make the quiet possible with their presence.
They put an end to panic moving through the night.
Nightjars encourage silence into happening.

## Being in the Presence

Being in the Presence is more than the here and now.
It is falling into the totality of silence;
hearing that secret personal message;
reaching from the mind to toes, a current of love;
shaking loose darkness
into pure light;
feeling lighter—a shuffling of belief.
It is then, and only then, we're transformed
into a cloud of welcoming birds.

## What Happens When in Stillness

There is a long walk from here to the pasture
where events are happening without you.
On the way, notice what you never did before.
Wait for the moment of no sound. You will hear this,
the under-breath of reverberation.
Stillness will stir the winds into heartbeats.
Wait patiently as a mountain shoving against clouds.
Wait until movement stops, which is impossible.
Wait for when the impractical becomes expected.
Remain in this emptiness. This is when you are in
the presence of anticipation. This is being within
unspoken prayer. This is what it is like to be flame.

# What It Is Like to Go into Silent Meditation

There were crabs and small fish in a hollow tidal pool.
Their life was fleeting temporary memories
into the left-behind, struggling into quietness.

How many of us feel this ultimate frustration—
that we are abandoned? But sometimes, winds return
from a place I can barely imagine.

How uncontrolled life is. How arbitrary it is:
moon-pull or merciless jury; stone heart or mercy. Which?
In the quest of meditation, the heart rests at a dangerous level.

There is a risk of not returning when we go this deep—
into a silence of our own choosing. There is the unnatural
amazement of letting loose and returning to an unchanged world.

## There Is Quietude

there is quietude      a planned whisper
in small soft voices
no one is supposed to hear

not even the best of us can hear these finest whispers
not even if we lower our ear too close to them
not when all noise is shut out

not if every wing-buzz was silenced
not even if every leaf stopped sobbing
not if the rocks abandoned their worry

for the garden snail inside its fist of a shell
like a doubt    like a poem needing revision
has tiny messages to say

whether the bee is not thinking of verses
when it composes its honeycombs or its queen
recites haiku       only the snail can say

# In the Beginning We Tumble into Light

> "In the beginning was the conversation"
> —Erasmus' translation of *John 1:1*

In the beginning we tumble into light.
We communicate in basic sounds
to express our needs. We need light,
yet we sleep and nourish. Our frailness
makes tenderness and care possible.
Our imprint of wailing need is constant
and dependent. This is never forgotten,
yet outgrown. Our small reaching arms,
our tracking eyes, test what sounds
evoke and which are ignored.
Sound is foreign and learned, mimicked
and memorized, cause and effect passed
from child to parent sharing common need.
From soundlessness to combining sounds,
making engagement, words are both archeology
and expansion. Communication is the beginning
of misunderstanding. We are embodied in language.

This is why it is so hard to talk with you.
Your words engaged our beginnings.
It should be easy as light and sound.
We should start with endlessly talking,
never running out of words to say or share,
or questioning, fishing for answers in shallow streams.
Let it always be this easy. It is as easy
as finding secrets in an acorn among the wordlessness.

Silence is waiting to speak,
from the beginning, when all messages were said,
on the ledge of awe.

# How Plain and Simple the Words, How Complex the Understanding

1.

"Whoever discovers what these sayings mean
will not taste death."
—Jesus, according Thomas, *Dead Sea Scrolls,* saying #1

How plain and simple is the world. Yet complex
as a spiders' web, or rocks only goats can climb.
What we know, others may not.
What we see, others cannot. Who among us
has known, seen, tasted, and heard all there is?
Not one, I say, plainly and simply. Not one understands.
When we are burning inside to tell what we know,
we quench it with indecision and fear.

And I heard,

if a bird ate out of your hand, you would not know why.
If I told you any plainer, you would still not understand.
If the sky was to write the answer, you would not look.
If you glanced upon the writing, it would not speak to you
in a way you would comprehend. Such is the lack of vision.
Such is the deafness to everyone shouting.
Such is the way of foul odors until it is too late.
Who among you has noticed the leaves wanting your attention?
Who has heard the silence and misunderstood it?

All of the earth is bringing us messages
of such depth. Because we do not listen,
those messages go through one end of the earth
straight to the other side
like drawing a thread through a needle.
Still, we look puzzled.
Confusion is a wind where there is no air.

                    And again I heard,
do I need to make it clear as a window into darkness?
Are my words not figs, but instead die on the vine?
How many times must I whisper inside your blood so it moves?
If I knock on your door, and you open it just the slightest,
is it because you do not see me? Or is it because you see me
and do not want to know me? Or is it some other fear,
like the fear of hearing what you do not want to hear,
because you prefer lies to my terrible truths?
I swear, if you were to silence me, the truth would still seep in.
It would slide under the door casing, or through the window slat,
or sieve through the moonlight, or tunnel through your feet.

Plain are my words, but to you they are murky and confounding;
you try to see more into their meaning or see less in them.
This is why you struggle like a person reading ancient runes.
Why not be simple and just listen? If my words reverberate
inside your lungs long enough, you will only breathe clean air.


                            2.


              "Know what is in front of your face and what
                  is hidden from you will be disclosed.
              There is nothing hidden that will not be revealed."
              —Jesus, according to Thomas, *Dead Sea Scrolls,* saying #5

Do you not see who prepares the way?
Does only a blind person see in darkness?
Only the one who can recite by rote dares to speak without regret.

When a bird hatches, it knows it is intended to fly.
When children are born, they grow older, forgetting what they knew at birth.
You are born with a great gift—do not forget it.

Study instead the mystery of the unknown until it reveals itself
blushing like a bride on the first night with a groom.
When you hear the hush after a wave finds a shore, that will be me.

When you look at your hands, what do you see?
When I look at mine, I see right through them into the heart of mysteries.
I see even the smallest, most unknown belongings.

Look again. Now what do you see?
If you still see insignificance, then you will always see a void.
If you stare long enough, you might see All.

What is greater? The seed, or what follows after?
You might ask why it matters when they follow each other.
It is this lack of understanding that keeps you from moving.

And for whom do you pave the way to understanding
when you do not understand yourself? It is better for a bird
to get lost in the skies than for it to fall from the heavens.

## Waiting in the Clearing

Waiting in the clearing,
what is clear?

The apricot blossoms open,
closing the valves of their hearts.

Loss never empties light completely.
Solitude is never silent enough to lose light.

Awareness always forgets.
When One speaks, no one knows what to say.

When life seems ending,
it is just beginning.

That which has been touched
must desire that feeling again and again.

When I untangle one truth,
a hundred more lies are exposed as wingless.

What light exposes, darkness tries to cover.
What comes goes even faster.

# This Pond Has Clear Imaginings

The pond wants to empty itself
of all earthly concern, to reach
a unique, passing insight,

a clarity, unspoiled by carp or
freckled tadpole, splaying across
the water in long, lingering laziness.

It wants more of itself, more purity
of the divine, the inspired,
to be thoughtful and thought-provoking,

to *twingle* when disturbed, to blush
when reflecting upon a sunrise,
to stand perfect as a heron becoming light.

It wants seven impossible changes
before waking; it yawns serenely,
holding its own breathlessness.

## A Door Felt Opening

I felt, rather than heard, a door close.
No one entered or exited, twice.
No wild sense of misery. No sloping star.
No tingling veins of air. Then, what?

No sparks of hearts murmuring in distance.
No Orion rising over the singing horizon.
No angels woken from slumber.
No from where thorn and morning glory meet.
Then, where? Where will I find what I can't?

Not under the robe of night. Not in quivering light.
Not in unseen sounds. This, I should investigate.
What is not here goes elsewhere.
We only get one chance to respond—
then, what we want most leaves.

# Psalm

Whenever I never know what to say to you,
compassion becomes a torrent of mountain rain.
The silence afterwards is incomprehensible.

In the room of stillness,
the separation between darkness and light
is writing a message on my heart.

I trace the etching with a finger.
Its grove is gouged from pressing so hard,
impressing its importance as on a stone tablet.

A strange echo of loons crosses water-light.
It is the abandonment of rushes in marsh grass,
the disturbances felt in wing-spread.

These disturbances go on even when no one sees them.
I would translate what they mean to the milkweed—
but silence is always here.

White birches rift in sinew winds. All twist
in fifths through twenty minutes of improvisation,
searching for the right grace note, that perfect pitch.

Peace is not found in the swells, or rowboats of clouds,
nor in the nave of a church where the choir practices.
All permanence is shaken as the sensitive bush shrivels.

All belief is taken. We do not seem to care.
The music is gone as white wings of breath.
We never understand the dark underside of clouds.

# Lamentation

You have forgotten my name.
You no longer call out to me for help.

I cannot find your voice intensifying from the earth.
I bury my sorrow into a seed as musical notes of despair.

My son, my son, you toss white sheets of death over my name.
I remove stones from my heart.

There is no comfort in this kind of planting.
There is no comfort in being tired afterwards, either.

My son, you have forgotten my name.
The ground is as torn up as I am.

# Psalm

There are so many disturbances on your face;
let me calm them.
Let me walk into your turbulent center.

I will bring with me news
to gladden your heart—
soap to cleanse your worry.

I am walking into your face
like an unknown song.
Know me.

# Listen

There are days when we should be outside,
in the map of fields, trying to locate the whelks,
the poppy sunrise, the ocean
of wild yellow roses, or the rabbit days
hurdling over the rise to where we have not been.
The world is rekindling its spirit.
It's happening without you.
You sit in the uncomfortable room
while the natural world is restoring its commitment.
Messages scuttle as hermit crabs. Birch trees
are mentioned in passing.

We cannot always enter yesterday like it is a cabin.
It is boarded up. The latch was never repaired.
The wire mesh screen door speaks softly about you.
It is in the pine scent of emptiness,
in the cupboards where not one memory is stored
except stillness.

What are you doing here when you can be out there?
You can fall halfway between dreams and never be
where you need to be. You need to find the deer-run.

If there is a wind, it is the same wind in the shape of weeds,
hunching over wildflowers. It enters you
as a flare of poetry, connecting ideas
you never imagined. Light strikes your face,
making it into a settling moon. Now listen.

## II. The Spiritual Journey

"Even though you're not equipped, keep searching: equipment isn't necessary on the way to the Lord."

—Rumi, *The Journey*

"And then alone in cold, light, open space, yet still deep within the mature erected form, a gasping for the clear air of the first one, the old one..."

—Rilke, *Imaginary Life Journey*

# Psalm

All day, inside me, your voice was saying
*wake up.* But *I* was not sleeping.

*Wake up,* you insisted. But I continued
to nibble at life.

At night, your voice would not let me sleep.
Someday I will rest, but not today.

I am stirring. Your voice is gnawing inside me.
I have been rowing in circles and did not know it.

# Misleading Spirits

A "daemon," according to Socrates, was a spirit who
would speak up when it was about to do something
not in accord with its true nature.

### 1.   Jesus

Once again, in the middle of sleep, he was possessed.
The rocks were chiding him in the desert
to walk off a cliff into trust.
Did this bring him closer to the Father? Or, to something else?
How do you approach the different angles of God?
How many are possible, and how many are impossible?
The notation upon his flesh declared: *find me!*
But where? The desert has no sign of God anywhere;
instead, it has the absence. Sleep is burning:
*Find me!* He is changing into bread.

### 2.   Buddha

What if, by preaching Emptiness,
you do not exist? You hollow out.
Words become light inside a dying lotus.
What if, by preaching, you become famous?
It would defeat the purpose of humility. And if
you become known in this life,
what happens in the next?
He thought of keeping the first idea silent
so the second idea would not be so disturbing,
but his first mind said, *tell people about finding!*

### 3.   Sitting Bull

He saw horses and men falling as stars, numerous
as grass, glowing, free-falling backwards, so many
he could not count them. He pulled back on the leather

as he danced a circle of increasing madness,
until barbs pulled chunks of incessant flesh from his chest,
yanking out dreams, feathers, horses of flame, arrows of stars.
He could hear the far-off voices wanting to know
what he had seen in his finding-vision. *Find me!*
called the crows. *Find me!* begged the long-yellow-hair.

### 4.    Ono no Komachi

Her numerous lovers were floating reeds shunning
the mountains in autumn. *How can you fail to see
the invisible?* Find me! *Indeed. Who am I to rest?
We are white eyebrows! We wear straw raincoats!*
Find me!

She was in the hiddenness, removing herself
until impermanence remained, and even then
she did not feel empty enough.

Kingfishers always find what they need
below reflection.

### 5.    Gandhi

Like making cloth from his own wheel,
he could make himself
thin as a moon, thin as last breath,
thin as a sliver in his finger,
make his breath small as leaf bud.

He went deep into silence,
its many rusty gates, its numerous absent breaths
past vision,
into pure light, into a trembling,
into subtle heartbeat.

All over, the twitching sky,
whorls of light from stars!

## 6.  Li Po

He would never find the light
at the bottom of the sea—
like rice wine, like Huron winging across shadows,
like stars falling out of his breath,
sudden stillness—

but he dove in anyway.

# The World Is Wildflower Boats

the world is wildflower
boats painted from water-washes
our needs allow us to believe

details of moonlight
and eating it
as wild mushrooms

like a hidden path
like tumbling piles of books
wind carries in its chest

words are calligraphy
dandelion puffs
from the empty boat of my body

a world of belief
where the hidden path
is finally revealed

## The Annunciation

Based on the painting by Van Eyke, 1434,
honoring *Luke I: 26-38*

*The Book of Hours* has been turned to the wrong stanza,
for I am not worthy.
I was in the temple, where I belonged,
working on a tapestry of prayer. Why have you chosen me?
You turn words at my unworthy feet.
Glories of seven rays come out of nowhere.
I am not special—just a pair of hands
stitching threads into cloth I am not worthy of making.
What is grace?
I do not embody it. I have no special permission.
I have no great words to speak. What is in my unworthy heart?
How can I bear such a burden? What is faith?
I am nobody,
less than a donkey hair, less than straw, less than a drop of rain.
You say I am illuminated. My hands only know thread,
the making of embroidery, casting useless seeds to doves.
What is praise? I am less than dust.
I work at the loom making a slip and readjusting.
Everyone notices my imperfections. I am less
than a beetle. Why am I compared to the setting of angels?
I notice all the Biblical images on the wall,
and I do not belong. Do not praise me.
I am humble as a thimble, or needle, or guiding thread.
I am full of alarm and uncertainty. Take back
this startling blue ermine. Take back praise.
Unbind this knot.
Do not honor me; I do not deserve it.
Do not extol me to be a host of stars.
Lend not my name to something I am not.
I am the furthest from glory.
I am the bend of light as it disappears.
I am common as a sparrow.

I am the draft from a window crack.
I am the wick flickering in no breeze.
I am the drip of wax.
I think, perhaps, you have mistaken me for someone else.
Someone not so common, not small as a ladybug.
I am soft spoken and have no sense.
You need someone fierce, someone flammable, someone unique
who does not sweep with a broom or collect water
from the lowest brook. I am not the one you seek.

# When the Angels Speak the Truth

their tongues are flames.

When they speak half-truths,
their tongues are a lake
without a ripple,
without a trace of doubt.

But when they lie—
and, oh my,
do they lie—

angels lie still.

∞

At 4 p.m., the angels of mercy
patrol the empty streets—

they carry themselves
like they were carrying baskets
of broken bricks

or anguish.

They come from a different
aberrant part of the backbone
where fish swim
in polluted air.

They come and they come
and they come,
endlessly, arriving
like it was the end we expected.

# Angel of Mercy

give me none.
My tribulations are mine,
brought on by my failures.
If there are places of regret,
I rent them.
If there are places of rest,
then I am evicted.
The angels shovel me out like coal,
me and my tongues of bankrupt prayers.
They point away
to where the horizon curves to no end.
Perhaps this is the point.
Perhaps this is my mercy.

∞

There is no beauty
in the angels of mercy.

When they open their grotesque mouths
like trumpets of doom,
locusts devour the land.

This is no beauty in this.
None.

∞

When there was newness,
the skin we owned
glowed like angels.

There was no need for mercy.
It already was
and then it was gone,
shedding.

The land quickens
with sadness.

## Tor House

Robinson Jeffers was sunning on granite,
lying skyward, composing on paper
the idea of rocks hewn into uneven squares,
because the world is not perfect. These rocks
would be the meditation of silence. They would
make an Irish castle with a turn-gate as a pathway
to walls of poems filled with hawk-joy, loam kisses,
lichen freckles, dizzy with word-blend.

The rocks would remember heron shadows,
concrete and isolated, in tune with nature
and heart. He would ask the rocks
for permission. He would carry them over the barrens,
beyond the periphery where surf collides with shore.

Over the promontory, he'd pass the outcrop of sea-grass
where the bitter place of winds coil and spring,
away from where water does not think
before it smashes. This house would become a lyric
of love, where to touch stone reminded him of love.

He would build low to the ground, to take the worst
of storm and loss. He would sing like terns in swoop
and sway, wheeling cursives of love in breakwater sky.
Granite walls would be in perfect pitch. He'd read aloud
into star-spray, use block-and-tackle lift. Not easy,
this work; not prideful either, the work of hands.
Where else could love feel the earthquake of heart?

## Looking in All of the Wrong Places

I found a simple tiny blue flower,
I proclaimed to everyone I met.
Some walked away, thinking I was crazy;
some listened intently, visualizing their own version
of a small blue flower, until they could smell it.
All listeners carried their messages to other listeners.
Soon, a whole garden of blue flowers
was everywhere,
including marigolds, periwinkles, irises, buttercups.

Tell me, after a long day of planting, that this was not important;
I have seen their eyes buzzing.
What we leave behind is just as important as what we take.

What will you plant today?

## How to Write Spiritually

A voice instructed, *Write paradoxes*
*not even you can untangle*
*if you had a thousand hands*
*under thousands of aimless suns. No,*
*write simply,* corrected the voice,
*as an ant carrying more than its own weight*
*in a line of numberless ants each carrying*
*more impossible weights. No, write*
*in the middle path, elusive as a butterfly*
*traveling to a place only generations of memory*
*remember, and if they die, interrupted on the journey,*
*it is all right. No, do not write daydreams.*
*By the time one thought enters like a first-night bride,*
*her lover has aged. No, be active so everyone knows*
*what is buzzing inside your hornet-nest heart. No,*
*everything has passed. What was written*
*is already erased. There is sap from a broken limb*
*already coalescing—you missed it—*
*a flight of rain has departed without you.*

# Exodus

Exodus is both a leaving and a journey towards
an unknown, into a trust
life will be better, a packing-up
and deciphering what to leave behind—
like footprints or archeology of our past,
planning with a map unfolding like umbrellas.
We risk traveling into the unknown without a plan,
sometimes in a rush, avoiding a disaster from weather,
or earth, or wars, carrying only what little we can.

Then the movement—the stop-and-go tiredness
and needing to rest, replenishing,
carrying through with a destination and perhaps
adjusted arrival time, transient and unnerved,
because travel takes longer than we expect.

What if we are refused entry? Stopped at a border crossing,
digging furtively or wrapping our hands
so as to get over razor wire and under erratic spotlights,
shot at and perhaps winged, limping as they follow
our blood trail like a hunter follows deer spoor.

Is this what we expected? Does the rain fall differently?
Does it have exceptional color? Was the trip worth it?
Was it more trouble than it was worth?

The process of self-evaluation occurs
if we make a journey or not. It happens
in the planning stages when we are most likely to question
ourselves and our motives. The specific outcomes
can never match the end result.

If settling in is possible, how long does it take?
Is it as long as a person adjusting to retirement
after 50 years of the same routine? Is there clarity?

What if this journey was a spiritual one
and the spirit does not answer what we need.
Perhaps the spirit answers with rhetorical existential questions,
expecting us to reach our own spiritual growth.
Perhaps we get the answer we need
but do not know how to interpret or apply the answers.

What if we die along the way, get lost,
are waylaid, or decide to stay at a random location?
What if, when we arrive and decide it is better
than where we came from, the grass is literally greener,
the birds are operatic, and the honey
has been mixed with strawberry pollen?

As we leave one question and enter into another
like a virus or an expatriate or a seeker or a guest,
is it the same uncertainty as giving birth or dying?
A leap of faith is needed more than faith itself.
The tendency to question is always present.
Our bodies are diasporas kindling fires within us,
ready to make do, aware another moving may be needed.

# Parable

A wind turbine on a hill
was not churning. Its aorta, clogged.
Its solitude was speechless

in stuckness. No spirit of breeze
to push against enormous blades,
like switchblades cutting the sky.

The wind was hibernating. Silence
caught in its throat, asthmatic.
Spuriousness was sunbaked. Heart

overreaching what little faith it had.
The winds returned,
stubbornly short of patience,

not seeking penance. And if
the wheel gained speed like a Sufi,
then what would pass?

What would be behind? Such is the labor
of love. Such is pain and loss. The cycle,
perpetually determined, in the same aimless pursuit.

Instead, be neither wind, nor blade, nor lost.
Be the one who does not need
in order to be in breathless light.

## It Is Written, We Must Forgive

It is written, we must forgive—yet forgiveness is impossible
to give or receive—it is easier to catch geese in flight—
and I flail at the exactness. How do you find words that are lost?

Loss is what I feel, when I fail or am failed.
How do I begin? How do I not? Where should I go
into the library of words—to find broken twigs of verbs?

Awareness is rising up—apologies from ashes of regret,
solemn as prayer—for prayer is what I have.
And you receive them—flutters of sighs wing out from you.

## Mending the Net

Based on the painting by Thomas Eakins, 1881

We gather as a community, prepared to mend.
Forgiveness is in the air.
If we do not restore trust, it will haunt us as a storm moving in.
The fabric of love demands patching.
We begin our solemn task, bent to this renovation.

We gather at *The Meeting Tree*—a place where we head
after a storm to make sure all is accounted for.
Anyone missing is a tangling of the net.
Let no one be lost. Anyone misplaced shall be found—
let not one body be mislaid.

We will spread our net far and wide.
We congregate at this wisp of a tree where our answers
are prayers. We inspect what we have made
and find it maddeningly wanting. There are gaps, rends,
some small as a gull's eye; some are bigger than grief.
The world cannot be repaired without hard work.
Listening to suggestions is the fishing of a religion.
Without a community, there is no sharing.

If we lack that, we swim as minnows within the silence.
We are making what was broken whole again.
Fishing has taught us patience.
We throw away what we do not need.

When someone is missing, we diminish into the accumulating loss.
We pursue a horizon as it stays far ahead,
uncertain as to when to haul in our cast nets.
We rely on instinct to stop and repair what is needed.

It is like knowing when to pray
and when it will not suffice. We are entangled
in the sharing, as words swim by too small for catching.
We are never done with mending promises in the sky-net.

# Psalm

Let go. Drift into release.
Into acceptance. Trust we will be all right.

This affirmation, this sureness of breath, is more
than words, more than a passing of one moment
into another.

The manuscript of conversion is written a chapter at a time.

There are more intervals, more stillness, to arrive.
What exactly is planned next?

There is a journey ahead without any plans,
with no certain destination,
where no future is written.

# Psalm

As close as any two molecules
of skin, I am to you.

During any uncertainty
of this truth, even when
you are not here,
you remind me—
love is that unusual.

Love is any number of birds
hiding in a winter bush
anyone can see;

when they take off,
it is like when you leave—
always that quickness.

As far away as you are now,
you are near.

Any impossibility
you are.

# I Am Ready!

I am ready!
I am ready for what is next!

What some think is wind
is inner light, finding
who is ready,
who is not.

Miracles are not
living through adversity,
heartache, sorrows, sickness;
do not look for them there.

Don't walk on a tightrope
to God. Nor circle like moths.
Nor feed many with one fish.

These are all fine.

But the true miracle
is what we do
with that blazing-ember heart
where either God is—
or is not.

I have been reading myself
to see that secret
behind the ancient curtain
a long time before time began.

Look!
It does not waver.

## III. Rapture!

"Kabir says this: When the Guest is being search for, it is
the intensity of the longing for the Guest that does all the work.
Look at me, and you will see a slave of that intensity."

—Kabir, *Ecstatic Poems* (2004), version by Robert Bly


"We should highly rejoice that God dwells in our soul
and still more highly should we rejoice that our soul dwells in God."

—Saint Julian of Norwich, *Infinite Love*

# Psalm

What happened to the middle years?
The restless birds are calling me.
I thrashed open the window,
tugged at the heart-strings of curtains.
I am tired of missed opportunities.
There are more questions than answers.
The light changes into a longing no one sees,
like a bee with its heavy load, asleep in my hand.
What am I waiting for?
If I had any prayers, I'd try not to forget them.
There is praise in the sunrise.
The world is waiting for my arrival.
The birds are reminding me the best they can.
It is up to me to respond. The singing begins inside,
a note building its ladder of light
to where I cannot see
into what I need to witness.

Let us go out—now!
A prayer can ride those notes,
up where birds spread a canvas of hymns.
Are you ready to sing?
I can hear your heart, your beloved heart,
ready to resonate.
We positively hum with expectation.

# Morning

the broken roof of sky
lets in limits of light
curtains of wind
remote sounds
from still countries
whispering living memories
remembering what we have forgotten

we are frail with having absorbed so much light
we could not hold anymore

# Psalm

How wonderful the Spirit—
the promise of the gladiolas
yellow in the enlightened air,
smelling new mysteries.

What I need is in the garden:
kneeling into the deepness of the ground
speaking to me through my palms
so my hands can see what the earth is telling me.

All I need is here, within reach:
the watering can full of delicious tears,
the purple pansies with their secrets,
the tiny wild strawberries taking over a stump.

I gather these into rain that is not raining. A song
of solace. A dance of fireflies like meteor showers.

I bring them to my nose, like bit garlic, inhale,
breathing like a desperate man, like a woman
who cannot get enough of the light.

So, here it is. I am sharing it with you.
It is the moon leaving its promises.
It is the shifting of the unknown.
It can have wings if it wants.

# Psalm

I cannot stop writing,
for this is written in my heart, leaping out!
I cannot stop.

If I did,
the messages would end,
my heart might fail,
the song from deep inside might dry up.

I cannot write fast enough;
my words are not necessarily my own.
The song is so deep,
so far from the belly,

it cannot possibly be from me.
The singing is so intense,
so much like fire, so fierce, so necessary,
I cannot quit.

If I pause, if I stammer in my rush of speaking,
if the words fly out of my fingers
faster than I can think, then what will happen
with all the words rushing out of my heart?

What singing still waits to be sung?
What voices still expect their turn?
My bones are humming; my body is a symphony.
What rising! What blissful rising of singing!

All because of you! All because
you fill me with such need
I am bursting, overflowing with singing
words so fast I cannot sing them fast enough.

It is almost exhausting. It is almost too much
for one person. Yet, it continues,
and I do not want to stop uncontrollable singing.
Let the music fill me with such fullness.

# Psalm

It is time to be intimate with
the world. Let the rooster wake
from his long languishing nap.
Let the world stretch as disappearing roads.
Let the birds bring the sky near as an embrace.

It is time to understand what I do not understand.
Clarity should be my tongue.
It should be in the fossilized rocks. In the wasp.
In the Johnny-Jump-Ups I pass on the highway.

I should hear the world as it is.
How the world will be from now on.

It is time to begin.

# Psalm

How can a broken heart be possible when we're enraptured?
There is information out there—explicit in all creation.

We are not required to be in contemplation
in order to obtain it. When we go into nature,
our senses are revived, replenished.

Belonging is messy, intrinsic business.
When we are in the presence of the Eternally Powerful—
engaged, comprehended—we are purified and illuminated.

# Psalm

Reacquaint ourselves with our surroundings.
Visit each day anew. A tremor comes at the occasional,

a movement not just for us, unless we search for it,
willing to share it—its hushed alertness.

Does the wonder shift the intention of creation,
forcing us to stop and observe what is there

all along—the meaning of what is, is here?
It is up to us to find the wonder and accept it.

Will we find the struggle? Or the survival?
Will we find that which will humble us?

The earth has its own way of speaking,
if only we hear it, even in its silence.

There are more than words to talk about the world.
There is reciprocal empathy.

We do not need our senses to assimilate the message.
We just know it; our hearts bursting, experiencing

the immanence and transcendence where Spirit lives.
We do not have to go far to get there.

Even the smallest sliver of ice contains this voice;
loss suddenly went into flame because of it.

## In the Presence of Absence

In the Presence of Absence we can find
our own lacking or our erasure.
Most people would hover around this loss,
a bottomless chasm,
but I leap in.

I can tell you this:
it does not go straight through earth
into the Endlessness.

There is no hard or soft landing. And for all I know,
I am still free-falling.

I feel hands under me, lowering me, gently,
all the while being told: *Trust.*
So I do.

I am no longer falling or rising; I am neither here,
or there, or anywhere.

I am in the Belonging, in the Longing;
I am accepted for who I am:
imperfect, curious, searching, believing.

## In Search of Everlasting Presence

How do we recover when the fields are ablaze?
What is before us?
Is this the evidence of everlasting Presence?

It is time to unravel the morning
to find the conflagration of possibilities
until the absence of an echo is gone from our hearts.

From our singing hearts,
there is this search for the divine.
Without the divine, there is
the unlimited Emptiness.

## The Incessant Knocking

Listen. The Lover is knocking,
but not on a door—in our hearts.
If we answer, what will we find?
If we sleep through the incessant knocking,
what will we miss?

When I first heard this tapping,
I opened the windows and shouted,
waking the robins, the dogs,
the moon, the crickets. Lights went on.
Everything was disturbed.

My secret Lover wished to be a secret,
so my Lover went away like a tidal wave,
like a dream.

The next time the Lover came visiting,
I was more prepared.
It was like finding light in a dark closet.

# Rapture

An assemblage of birds is hiding in its own calling.
Its music is in the raspberries.
Thick sheet music of fog hovers low to a changing ground,
while above is autumnal-harsh light.
The light's astonished response is to migrate.

It's unexpected, yet anticipated,
thumbing throughout the departure of days. This calling
is interwoven. It is damp and is memorized differently,
back to the way life used to be.

This unsung chattering continues
into redness of a cold morning.
There is emptiness afterwards,
piercing as the deep hill. It is tuneless.
In the low-sung air, there is a burn-off, unraveling.

Then, what is that calling? What use is it?
There is no umber sky being called forth.
Who speaks in silence? The ground flutters and flits.

Music is a waiting river, moving out of intense hunger.
Scarlet birds blend into bleeding, burnished skies.
Their shadows imagine songs impossible to sing. Once over,
it is over: a river roving on.

I believe this amber forest was always this red,
its leaves flapping. A clap of thunderheads
is a clump of teeming cardinals, slapping out of branches
up into the aggregation, dredging up brightness,
bristling with dew, releasing themselves from guilt into sunrise,
disintegrating into an epiphany, scattered as weather.

This is no normal awakening from silence into song.
A hush from the hickories was astonished in the afterlight.
It is in the blaze of foglift.

# I Have Lost My Way

We can get lost in snow, but not in your love.

In blinding whiteness,
your voice calls me into comfort.
In the avalanche of silence, you search for me.
In frost-bitten words, I do not know what to say.

My tracks disappear into falling snowstorm.
Yet you are ready to cover me with blankets
and rub my body into a conflagration of love.

I am in snowfall,
trying to find my way back out of whiteout.

Keep calling my name.

## IV. The Temporary World

"No sound of the mid-day bell enters this fastness where blue mist
rises from bamboo groves; down from a high peak hangs a waterfall;
none knows where he has gone, so sadly I rest, with
my back leaning against a pine."

—Li Po, *Visiting a Taoist on Tiatien Mountain*

"One night as I sat in quiet, I seemed on the verge of entering a world
inside so vast I know it is the source of all of us."

—Mirabai

"Be willing to be a beginner every single morning."

—Meister Eckhart

# The Universe Has a Sermon about Remembrance

If I could not hear,
the marshes would send their breezes
full of loons and drakes.
If I could not speak, silence would speak for me:
becoming yellow roses, incandescent star-falls,
grammar of memory,
adjectives of landscapes.

The world would not abandon me.
Love would be compound sentences
in traces of uncommon space.
I would know more than I do now.
I would know parables of love.

In this, there is no vacuum of oblivion.
There is only promise.

## Psalm

Come here, rest in my lap—until grass is wet memory,
until wind forgets and takes and returns
what never happened.

Come here, where ache rests, where leaves
use impossible colors, where perception of love
is in the translation—

this water has never tasted so good,
bees find all the sacred flowers,
the sky loses its tension.

Let me whisper in you.
Let the invisible shed into wide stances of air.

# Psalm

Just when I needed you,
a message, like forgotten dust,
settled in front of me, expecting
to be discovered and renew me.

Not just once, but several times—
and here is where it gets sketchy:
the message was clear,
but apparently no one else could read it.

I tried to show it to others, but the words
blurred because they were not intended
for everyone—so this is all I can share.
Is it enough? Will it abide?

# Questions in Unnecessary Rain

How secure are we
in the gathering of our autumns?
Is there another day
to make amends?

Maybe this day is all we get.
There is no more.
What if? What if we knew
*that* Reality was true?

Maybe, we would act differently
before it is too late
and the moment skates by.
Could we find the words?

Would those words come easy or hard
or intermittent as unsteady rain?
Would they stick
like a miner trapped in a collapsed cave?

I have no ready answer for this.
I tried prayer in an empty room, and no one listened.
Meanwhile, we can back-peddle away,
a moon going dark and never coming back.

## We Should Be Disturbed

We should be disturbed—
wanting to climb into cherry blossoms when it snows pink—

proclaiming love loudly in the throes of love,
a plaintive call from clouds.

The world should be full of noise,
shaking sleeves of night-shivers,

making a calligraphy of love,
a thrush sharing its four-notes to no one in particular.

In this constant creating,
the hibiscus moon is in a flock of star-swans.

## Psalm

There is a passing, calling me from somewhere.
My blood feels it—
starting over the wheat fields—like a hand.
This is an immediate transitory passage
from this world into the next world.
This is a loss that we cannot imagine.
At our quieter moments, we will hear this calling
and respond.

Will we be receptive to this calling?
Or will we continue to close our ears?
And if we look, what will we see?
Will we see what we are meant to notice?

It is impossible to ignore this calling.
We are in the forever.
Accept the emptiness of our hearts;
sing back to this calling. Enter into it,
feeling the weight of our own losses;

then, we are graced. Now turn
to enjoy the richness of living, fully.
Life is a long preparation of saying goodbye.
This inevitable leaving is what we all must do.

# Psalm

"How shall the heart be reconciled/ to its feast of losses?"
—Stanley Kunitz, *The Layers*

I have seen people die,
watching them turn into light,
catching it as they go
to a place so full of light
it can always take more.

I, too, want to hold light.

I have moved through continents of lives,
numb to the world around me,
forgetful of what is important.

Please remind me
if I ever forget again,
if I forget to appreciate what I have.

We slip in and out of life
like we were trying on shoes
to see which will fit us.

I, too, want to hold onto light
like it was air.

Whose cheek did I first touch?
What first unknown door did I open?

What did I leave behind?

If I leave one message behind,
let it be love.
Let it be an everlasting love
like tender rain in you.
Let it give you light to hold in your hands.
Let it be love.

# How to Recover from Loss into Light

"For me, everything was too much, and nothing was enough"
—Mary Karr, *Facing Altars: Poetry and Prayer*

What exactly is gracious or especially tragic
and unsung about a hurtling death?
We have enough troubles,
having wrung the essence out—
like getting out of bed with a cold, dehydrated.
Life is too much
but not enough of what is important;
never enough, never, never prayer—

ignoring small blessings; the scarce air;
the restless resonating tiny, inner voices:
rippling pebbles from the cauldron
of abundance. Never enough for us, but sufficient
to see the edge between *enough* and *not enough*—
a wedge between uncertainty and belief.

Instead—try filling, tossing earth upon earth,
filling *that* cavity in the heart. Try
dark earth, the kind earthworms prefer.
Try moss-smelling soil, enriched nitrate
fillings of dirt, rich as lavender soap. If that fails—
if we still feel like failure—try mud,
straw, dry crumbling leaves, compost,
rejection letters that litter the heart. Fill—
until it mounds, like fairy mounds
in Africa created by termites. Build monoliths
like Stonehenge slabs, teeth gnawing at light.
Construct ziggurats, towers for Nimrod, escape
limits of language into a frenzy of silence.
*Awe* is just too unnamable.

When our arms become the spade
mouthing absolute light and dirt,
toss more muck onto the pain.

# Psalm

"For God is not the author of confusion, but of peace"
—*I Corinthians, 14:33*

The last message we want to say before we die,
is we had love. Not always heart-thumping love.
Love may have eluded us,
or arrived unexpectedly,
but love nevertheless. Tender is the mercy
when we can say we loved and were loved.
Although, it was not always true we had love.
Love was not always abundant;
it was reckless, unpredictable, lacking,
and often unrealistic. Yet in spite of this,
love stayed, like an all-day drizzle,
and departed just as slowly. We are rich
or poor in love. We want to tell the truth
when we die—that sometimes love
was what we needed, and we had love
when we needed it most.
The truth of love is never known;
but the absence of love is always known.
It is important to acknowledge what we had
and despair when love is gone.

# After

No matter, burning darkness
or lack of indelible light, there are
always two kinds of unkind deaths.
Neither is silent restlessness
nor noisy orchids.

They are echo and lack of echo,
guilty annexes
where heart refused to listen:
two death-whispers
summoning.
Disorderly angels follow,
banging soft gongs. What remains
is silence, sweltering silence
burnt once by loss, seared twice
by memory, flailed skin.
What went away returns
lost in ruins.

# Early Autumn at Itako

Based on a woodblock by Kawase Hasui
(Note: *Itako* are blind shamans)

Our boat of ghostly rains merges deliberately
into a stream of darkness. It is a song
of settling-down, the kind a mother coos to her baby.

The river is messaged, and its skin ripples.
The moonlight is a part of this song.
Noise whispers across water as a dwindling star.

Let go of the oars. Let them slip into the evening,
and trust that you will be taken somewhere.
Lack of trust is ripples that fade.

The oar is already into the lost. We are barely moving,
and yet we are moving, like a mother swaddling a child
into a blanket of clustered stars.

What is the difference, when we are so loved,
that the wrapping takes the length of a song and not less?
The melody crosses a lake with the same current as moonlight.

When we grow older, our songs unravel their wrappings,
the boat lists, the stars are further from our cupped hands,
but our whisper is a mosquito heard in the absence of a lake.

What startling secret can we let drive in stilled water?
When a distant voice calls us to come home,
will we answer that plaintive cry?

# Waiting

I have been waiting
to spiral out of control
erasing what I know
taking me with it

I do not mind dying so much

I imagine being taken
is more like being yanked out
into an elsewhere

when the end comes
as vines climbing towards sunlight
it will be astounding
and I will have a front row seat

## Living in the Breathless Moment

living in the breathless moment

that moment of surprise

that heart-
break into silence

the no sound        the absolute hush
where this world folds into a pocket

I have been carrying this secret for a while
neither burden nor joy

this moment-to-moment
amazement of small messages speaking

it is too much love
none of which I believe I deserve

# An Invisible Weight

And there, for all of invisible weight
of gravity, are unspoken words
like a thousand hands.

In fullness of bird-song,
in the trembling emptying of branches,
we are disturbed by movements of silence.

Hands, more soil than flesh,
feel unspoken
turning over the necessary words.

And when those unknown hands lift,
the weight is no longer there,
or anywhere, anymore.

We do not have to think
how to enrich the soil of love.
We should always be tending, tending.

Our transient life is never completely aware
of its short existence.
We can be part of the listening stillness.

## Love Is Breathing

love      like music      is breathing
the deepest
memory or future or now or never
finds in air      where
nothing cares
what happens next
because it will happen
regardless

regardless of impressions
light or shadow
animals born out of expectant air
to changes we need to make
never too late
like a solid      forceful      wind
gives in
              to the greater force

before I die      O      I can say
I loved      was loved
regret was a shadow
in far off green fields
only a single step      gone
to a person in tremendous love
sinews of light

forgiven

# Psalm

All day my heart has been emptying!
When I think I cannot be sadder,
reaching the bottom of sorrow is endless,
is draining. When I think there is no sadness left,
more of me departs as flights of melancholy herons.
And still the gnashing heart wails like dying leaves.
There seems to be no end to the loss: the absence of stars
on the darkest lung of night. When will you return?
My fingers ache for you. My eyes search the horizon
for movement, the slightest breeze of you.

## The Singular Moment

The quickening unfolds—
a nightingale sings a peach blossom
from invisible stillness.

No one is permeable. Nor any life.
Leaves turn brittle, rain
dries, a soundlessness
of birds fly tremendous distances.
Rocks break into light. Bells forget how to ring
inside a chrysanthemum.

The singular moment when we are alive
does not have to make sound
in order to cause amazement.

# Message

we are waiting for a message
that never comes       impatient for the Spirit
to lift the day    like a small child into open arms of sky

we face silence
                        loneliness is overwhelming
we find no welcoming place

why does the heart not feel open
          the sky is not the face of silence
enter           instead          into the overwhelming

Spirit has wanted to share this message
      all in the universe is fine
Spirit has known us since we were born

the answer is in the Silence
          we have not been listening
so we do not know it       we do not feel welcomed

we are searching for the message
in the wrong places       impatience cannot find Spirit
Spirit's heart of waterfalls is overwhelming

like doors of butterflies       like jars of laughter
Spirit
has been waiting for us

light will split our chests open
breaking clouds over anvils
banging gongs

## When Stillness Is Heard

There was no one there when I heard a voice.
Haven't you had a strangeness like this?
I did not respond right away, ignoring it,
and its restlessness increased.
I chucked it off as imagination.
Haven't you ignored queasy feelings?
Perhaps it was from the empty fields.
But there was stillness in the grass and air.
This uneasiness followed me into the car
and went with me.
The stillness was so quiet.
There was silence in my house.
No sound in the sky. Emptiness in the isolated miles.
The voice persisted.
Ever ignore a message that refused to be ignored?
It was telling me to *enjoy* and *love*.
That message was everywhere it needed to be.
All I had to do was *listen*—then, it was everywhere.

# Acknowledgments

*Ancient Paths:* "The Incessant Knocking," "Waiting in the Clearing"

*Bagel Bard #6* (anthology): "Psalm: There is a passing, calling me from somewhere"

*Bagel Bards #9* (anthology): "A Door Felt Opening"

*Big River Review:* "How Plain and Simple the Words, How Complex the Understanding," "Tor House"

*BlazeVOX:* "Psalm: I have seen people die"

*Blue Heron Press:* "Living in the Breathless Moment," "The Singular Moment," "Message"

*Centrifugal Eye:* "Misleading Spirits"

*Cherry Blossom Review:* "Morning" (originally published as "the broken roof of sky")

*Flutter Poetry Journal:* "Looking in All of the Wrong Places," "In the Presence of Absence," "Psalm: All day, inside me, your voice was saying," "We Should Be Disturbed"

*Furnace:* (as three untitled poems) "There is quietude, a planned whisper," "How wonderful the Spirit," "It is time to be intimate with things"

*The Gift of a Rose* (anthology): "Psalm: The last message we want to say before we die"

*The Gospel According to Poetry* (anthology): "Psalm: Just when I needed you"

*Istanbul Literary Review:* "Listen," "How to Be Silent"

*Journey Planner & other stories & poems* (anthology): "How to Recover from Loss into Light"

*Mandala Journal:* "Exodus"

*Masque of the Red Death:* "Parable"

*Meditations on Divine Names* (anthology): "Angel of Mercy," "When the Angels Speak the Truth," "In the Beginning We Tumble into Light"

*Napalm and Novocain:* "After"

*Numinous:* "Untitled (Being in the Presence is more than the here and now)," "Psalm: Let go. Drift into release," "When Stillness Is Heard," "Psalm: Reacquaint yourself with your surroundings"

*Parting Gifts:* "Psalm: Why do things arrive late?"

*Poetica Magazine:* "In Search of Everlasting Presence"

*Poetry in the Cathedral* (anthology): "What Happens When in Stillness"

*Poppy Road Review:* "The World Is Wildflower Boats"

*Punkin House Digest* (anthology): "Psalm: I cannot stop writing"

*Reaching Out & Other Stories & Poems* (anthology): "Questions in Unnecessary Rain"

*Red Poppy Review:* "What it is like to go into Silent Meditation"

*Rhubarb:* "It is written, we must forgive"

*Soul-Lit:* "Psalm: Come here, rest in my lap," "Untitled (as close as any two molecules)"

*Strange Girl blog:* "*The Annunciation*"

*Traveling Poets Society* (anthology theme "Love"): "*Mending the Net*"

*The Wayfarer:* "I Have Lost My Way," "Lamentation"

*The Whirlwind Review:* "How to Write Spiritually"

*Wilderness Literary House Review:* "Rapture," "Psalm: The universe has a sermon about remembrance," "Psalm: How can a broken heart be possible when you're enraptured?"

*Written River:* "This Pond Has Clear Imaginings," "*Early Autumn at Itako*"

"How Plain and Simple the Words, How Complex the Understanding" won the *Big River Poetry Review* William K. Hathaway Award for Poem of the Year 2012.

"I Am Ready!" and "Love Is Breathing" appeared in "Dedication" (a minichapbook by Origami Poetry Press.

"Tor House" was nominated for Poem of the Month: August 2013, and for a 2013 Pushcart prize, by *Big River Poetry Review*.

*Cover artwork, "Sun, Water, Cold" by Pete Linforth; author photo by Linda Griggs; cover and interior book design by Diane Kistner; Charter text with Ocean Sans titling*

## About FutureCycle Press

FutureCycle Press is dedicated to publishing lasting English-language poetry books, chapbooks, and anthologies in both print-on-demand and ebook formats. Founded in 2007 by long-time independent editor/publishers and partners Diane Kistner and Robert S. King, the press incorporated as a nonprofit in 2012. A number of our editors are distinguished poets and writers in their own right, and we have been actively involved in the small press movement going back to the early seventies.

The FutureCycle Poetry Book Prize and honorarium is awarded annually for the best full-length volume of poetry we publish in a calendar year. Introduced in 2013, our Good Works projects are anthologies devoted to issues of universal significance, with all proceeds donated to a related worthy cause. Our Selected Poems series highlights contemporary poets with a substantial body of work to their credit; with this series we strive to resurrect work that has had limited distribution and is now out of print.

We are dedicated to giving all of the authors we publish the care their work deserves, making our catalog of titles the most diverse and distinguished it can be, and paying forward any earnings to fund more great books.

We've learned a few things about independent publishing over the years. We've also evolved a unique, resilient publishing model that allows us to focus mainly on vetting and preserving for posterity the most books of exceptional quality without becoming overwhelmed with bookkeeping and mailing, fundraising activities, or taxing editorial and production "bubbles." To find out more about what we are doing, come see us at www.futurecycle.org.

# The FutureCycle Poetry Book Prize

All full-length volumes of poetry published by FutureCycle Press in a given calendar year are considered for the annual FutureCycle Poetry Book Prize. This allows us to consider each submission on its own merits, outside of the context of a contest. Too, the judges see the finished book, which will have benefitted from the beautiful book design and strong editorial gloss we are famous for.

The book ranked the best in judging is announced as the prize-winner in the subsequent year. There is no fixed monetary award; instead, the winning poet receives an honorarium of 20% of the total net royalties from all poetry books and chapbooks the press sold online in the year the winning book was published. The winner is also accorded the honor of being on the panel of judges for the next year's competition; all judges receive copies of all contending books to keep for their personal library.